Table of Contents

Christopher Jon Bjerknes

Intelligent Morality

Chapter One
The Road to Hell Is Paved With Good Intentions

The worst and most enduring tragedies and catastrophes in a person's life are often the result of someone's mistaken attempt to do Good, even our own. Many have wished for a time machine so that they could travel back in time and reverse a horrible mistake they made with the best of intentions. Few seek to better educate themselves and create information systems documenting their mistakes to prevent future calamities. How many work to improve the general competency of everyone in society so that fewer Evil blunders are made and consistently better outcomes are achieved across the entire spectrum of life? Intelligent Morality proposes to attain this goal.

The ultimate tragedy, the complete destruction of humanity in the name of God, is being engineered and is likely about to occur. We need to prepare for the Apocalyptic mass attack the supposedly divinely inspired revealed religionists are planning to perpetrate against us. They are trying to destroy the Earth and all human life but a small remnant of their own which they plan to transform into androgynous beings that cannot accurately be described as "human".

A new moral code is needed to replace Revealed Religion, one which will enable a remnant of normal human beings to survive and thrive in the event the apocalyptic messianic revealed religionists succeed in their plans to exterminate most of humanity and really do inflict their staged Apocalypse upon us. We can't save everyone, but that should not stop us from saving ourselves and preparing to build a new world out of the ruins others will leave behind after they are exterminated due to their failure to prepare and inability to defeat the enemy. This plan for a New Society will be treated much more fully in later chapters.

There is also a moral imperative to improve parenting skills, reduce medical malpractice, up the skills, techniques, knowledge and ability of the trades and professions, produce better friendships, relationships and marriages, etc. but few understand that. Failures in all these areas and countless others are extremely costly and produce Evils that haunt everyone's lives, yet there is no broad societal recognition that it is fundamentally immoral to permit such incompetence and negligent failure. Instead, the excuse is often made that despite causing terrible harm or death, the person who harmed someone else or themselves meant well and learned a lesson.

That pointless excuse is considered the moral resolution to the dilemma of preventable failures and reckless injuries made by people who intended to do Good, or at least did not mean to do harm. Evil is also unproductively attributed to God's will or Satan's mischief, which delusions circumvent a scientific analysis of what actually occurred when tragedy strikes, how to keep it from happening again, how to achieve the desired outcome and whether or not the goal set is truly Good or inherently Evil.

Logical conclusions alone, or the presumption of divine revelation alone, is not enough to prove the ability of a given moral standard to produce Good or Evil outcomes. Tested knowledge of what will work and what won't to produce the intended outcome is vastly superior to Revealed Religion in producing predictably Good results. Revealed Religion is often counterproductive because it misleads believers into thinking their Good intentions will receive divine intervention to produce Good results. Their misguided assurance, arrogance and complacency can maim, kill or otherwise destroy lives.

The Intelligently Moral person pursues knowledge and approaches decisions with skepticism and the awareness that they are fallible even though they fully intend to do Good. Nothing prevents a religious person from acting in this same way, but they are less prone to do so if they believe the Gods promote Good and oppose Evil, or that they are in a battle against and must overcome Evil forces instead of ignorance, ineptitude, misguided and false beliefs, poor advice and bad choices.

Logical statements and tradition must be tested under repeatable circumstances to determine whether they are in fact true or false under those conditions. Aristotle logically concluded that heavier objects fall faster than lighter objects *in vacuo*, but Galileo's experiments on the Leaning Tower of Pisa falsified that logical conclusion and experimentally demonstrated that all masses fall at the same rate of acceleration in a vacuum.

Christianity asserts the allegedly divine revelation that it is Good for the Soul to turn the other cheek when struck and for the Christian to assume that there is neither Male nor Female, Greek nor Jew, but such self-destructive and undignified assertions are demonstrably false and do not withstand the test of experiment, yet they remain unalterable falsehoods that the Christian simply disobeys in order to survive, or perishes in their fruitless pursuit of immortality and martyrdom by mistakenly believing they are morally Good and divinely inspired to ruin themselves.

Countless medical doctors have murdered their innocent patients intending to do Good by trying to heal them with Evil treatments or withholding or neglecting to provide Good treatments. Good intentions alone are not enough to produce Good results and the mythical Gods do not intervene to ensure otherwise, nor do they punish Evil acts whether committed with the Evil or Good intent of the perpetrator who inflicts harm. Mythical Gods will not ensure that a person who intends to do Good will of necessity do Good or prevent them from mistakenly doing Evil.

The mythical Devil will not prevent a person who intends to do Good from doing Good nor tempt them to do Evil. Parents can ruin their children's lives with entirely Good intentions, as for example in the case of a move to a new house and change to a new career that ends up in disaster because of the delusions of the parents that this new way of life will benefit them, or their failure to properly assess the condition of the house, the neighborhood or the future of the economy and their new career. Lovers who are a poor match often destroy one another with the best of initial intentions.

The intent to do Good is not even a necessary condition for doing Good, though it is certainly often helpful for achieving Good results. Machines incapable of bearing Good or Evil intentions and the randomness of general events can often produce Good or Evil results, including yielding a good crop from good weather, or effectively or ineffectively braking an automobile barreling down the road towards a pedestrian.

Someone who intends to do Good needs the knowledge, skills, willingness to act, information, assessed data, experience, training, ability, sound judgement, etc. which are likely in all probability to produce Good. The best witch doctor cannot cure an infection with an incantation of supposedly divinely inspired words. Likewise, the best modern physician often murders his or her patient with the best of Good intentions because they lack a good solution due to there being none known, attempted treatments which are incorrectly thought to help but instead injure, ignorance of a good remedy which is known but just not known or is rejected by the physician, misdiagnosis, mistakes, following recommended procedures that are in fact fatally flawed evil policies, following bad advice, working outside of their specialty or experience, prioritizing treating one patient over another, etc.

The nonextant Gods do not reward Good intentions with Good results nor can they promote Evil. To compensate for the reality that the Gods do not reward Good behavior, the story of *Job* in the Bible teaches that being a righteous person is not a guarantee of heavenly rewards or assistance. The Old Testament instead instructs the Israelites that those who fail to do Evil are foolish prey of those who do practice Evil for their own benefit.

The worst Evil to enter into any given person's life is often perpetrated by people intending to do that person Good. Doctors can scar a newborn for life or kill it with an improper delivery or treatment. Parents often intending to benefit their own children often hurt, harm or kill them, frequently because they are following bad advice, incorrect dogmas, destructive cultural traditions, etc. Many of these instances were entirely preventable if only sound scientific moral standards were applied and the knowledge of what to do had been available and used. Tested knowledge is often a far more moral means of achieving Good than supposedly Revealed Religion. A doctor will have a much better chance of doing Good if he or she is equipped with proper knowledge and techniques, than with a Bible, cross or a medical book that is filled with falsehoods and myths.

The Gods will not intervene to ensure that a Priest serving Communion with the best of intentions will not pass Herpes from one congregant to another, or that a physician who fails to properly wash his hands will not infect his next patient. Good and Evil are produced by the laws of causality and circumstances, not the Gods. There are scientific means to act with the greatest probability of Good success and intent is only the start, not the be all and end all of generating moral outcomes.

Intent merely initiates action to achieve a desired outcome, it does not in and of itself necessarily cause that outcome. The physical world is governed by measurable properties and testable laws. A computer that is able to assess supplied data and produce an intelligible statement that serves as a recommendation can potentially do Good where an inept, incompetent, misunderstanding, ignorant, misguided, stupid, deluded, intoxicated, dogmatic, erroneous, etc. parent or friend with the purest of intentions to do Good can harm, maim or kill a person and the Gods will not guide them, stop them, punish them or inhibit them from doing so.

A belief in divinely Revealed Religion creates an unrealistic and destructive expectation that Good intent creates of itself Good results and Evil intent creates of itself Evil results. The results are purely determined by the actions or withholding of actions of the persons involved and the physical laws of Nature, as well as the happenstance of circumstances. The probability of success can be increased by access to knowledge, especially tested knowledge, advanced logic, cumulative data, good ideas, proper methods and means of assessing data, experimentation, cumulative experience, etc.

Often very successful families and societies continue to succeed because they share accumulated experience and knowledge across generations which has stood the test of time. They devote time and resources to educating their children and carefully monitor their children's friendships, relationships, teachers, education, etc. and provide them with the knowledge and advice that is likely to produce Good outcomes. Good advice can save a person's life or prevent them from making a tragic mistake like marrying the wrong person, buying the wrong house or following bad medical advice. Blaspheming the Gods cannot harm a person other than inciting Evil people to harm them for the supposed offense, but choosing to walk across obviously slick ice after saying a prayer and falling and breaking one's spine can ruin a life or take it.

No one is entitled to or will receive Good outcomes by supernatural means. They can only be brought about randomly or by proper actions. Bad choices made with Good intentions often produce far more Evil results than deliberately Evil acts. The worst and most harmful events to destroy a person's life are often the product of misapplied Good intentions. Proper and expansive tested knowledge can often do infinitely more Good than a talisman cross or magical Bible, or expensive but false education at the supposedly best schools that dogmatically preach flawed and harmful beliefs.

Chapter Two
Which Better Serves Us, Science or Faith?

One of the greatest defects of Revealed Religion is the misguided and false expectation that Good intentions are enough to produce Good results because the Gods supposedly intervene on our behalf to guide and help us. Most religious moral doctrines teach that Evil results from Evil forces and from people intent on committing Evil acts.

The truth is that many of the most Evil acts are committed by people who intend to do Good but lack the knowledge, skills and experience to accomplish their goals in a realistic, tested and proven manner. The victims of these catastrophically Evil, though unintentionally destructive acts perpetrated by people who are out to do Good, but who fail due to their ignorance, incompetence or misguided beliefs, are often loved ones of the individual or group which is sincerely trying to do Good. The nonexistent Gods never intervene to prevent harm from coming to those who follow the imaginary Gods' laws while devoutly and sincerely intending to do Good, or those whom the religious seek to help in ways that are actually self-defeating, destructive, harmful and horrendously Evil.

This is, of course, also true of the non-religious. They are also prone to hope that their Good intentions will produce Good results due to their intent alone and are often at least as lax as the religious in ensuring to the best of their ability that their methods and actions are sound and tested and will NOT do harm. They, too, are prone to falsely believe that something is Good which is actually Evil.

A father who rewires an electrical outlet in his home with the intent of doing Good and making it safer for his family may instead set fire to his house and kill his own children, which is clearly a terribly Evil act, but is not recognized as such by Revealed Religion. Someone who moves and changes jobs with the Good intention to better his or her lot in life but unwittingly purchases a horrendous house in a bad neighborhood can ruin the lives of his entire family, which is obviously and definitionally Evil.

Bad decisions, advice, choices, practices, relationships, friends, relatives, etc. are often the worst source of Evil in a person's entire lifetime, though the calamities they produce are mistakenly portrayed as if the result of merely misguided or wrong behavior in retrospect simply because the person or group responsible intended to do Good. Smoking, drug abuse, disease-inducing and relationship ruining promiscuity and other such vices are recognized as Evil and sinful by both Intelligent Morality and most Revealed Religions, though the Revealed Religions are being corrupted to deny the Evil nature of these behaviors which so often ruin lives.

Though Revealed Religion focuses on battling Evil as if it were a supernatural force and punishing those who deliberately seek to do Evil, it usually neglects to develop the knowledge and skills which would enable its adherents to consistently achieve Good outcomes and to test and observe what is actually Good and what is truly Evil in the real world as opposed to the immutable dogmatic religious abstractions iterated by Revealed Religions. Instead of relying upon scientific methods and continuous experience, Revealed Religion instead creates the illusion that the Gods will intervene to ensure that those with Good intentions will achieve their goals and produce Good outcomes if they help the Gods to fight Evil by obeying the Gods and their laws. According to the religious, the Gods supposedly have taught humanity what is Good and humans need only follow these arbitrary rules and Good will automatically ensue in all they do as fulfillment of the contract between the guardian Gods and their human slaves. Revealed Religion falsely teaches its followers to believe that the righteous are automatically rewarded and infallible, and the wicked are hindered and destined for punishment if only in the afterlife.

In the pursuit of Good, the religiously minded person is often encouraged to pray, to shun Evil—even Evil within him or herself, to engage in superstitious rituals and practice magic, and to have faith that the Gods have provided these magical means for success which automatically produce Good results through obedience to the will of the Gods. Revealed Religion does not generally provide a realistic, tested, fact based or data driven assessment of what constitutes Good and Evil in the long term. It does not provide a practical means of obtaining the goals and standards it sets other than by compelling obedience to its arbitrary laws. Reliance on faith, prayer, superstitious rituals and magic does not realistically or necessarily afford the religious person the tools needed to bring about the actual Good they intend to do or a practical means of deciding what really is Good and what Evil for them and their descendants, especially over the course of thousands of years. Is it really morally Good to open your borders or fight some other country's wars just because a "holy" book tells you to?

In practice, Revealed Religion promotes the myth that one needs to focus on fighting Evil as the primary method of producing Good and neglects to encourage the development and use of scientific methods of determining and achieving that which has been tested, assessed and shown to be Good. There is little to no acknowledgment of the fact that a tremendous amount of Evil comes from those meaning to do

Good, but who instead cause horrific harm and terrible Evil including the genocide of millions. The Gods are trusted to prevent these Evil outcomes, instead of people employing logic, data collection and assessment and the scientific method, as well as their conscience, to determine what is Good and how best to achieve it in predictable and proven ways. When things turn out badly, it is fatalistically attributed to the will of the Gods or Satan, not the failure of the religiously righteous to achieve their desired results through religious methods.

The ultimate goal of morality is to produce Good and Revealed Religion often obstructs the ability to achieve Good outcomes by distracting and deluding those who follow it by teaching them that there are supernatural forces which will guide and assist them to inevitably produce Good results if they merely intend to do so. When the religious fail at their task, they are taught to attribute their failure not to their own failings and delusions and the failings and delusions of their religion, culture and society, which can at times be instructive and productive, but to the will of the Gods or the intervention of Evil forces. Dogma stands in the way of their ability to do Good and often compels them to do Evil.

Such mythological beliefs are not a practical means of determining and creating Good and instead tend to produce Evil through a lack of applied knowledge, training, learning, adaptation, action and intelligence. A good idea and hard work is often what is needed to do Good, not merely a good intention. Revealed Religion most often fails to take this fact into account and fosters the false and defeating belief that Good intentions alone are enough to produce Good results because the Gods have supposedly made the world that way and will ensure it continuously functions that way. Religious cosmology, ontology, epistemology and metaphysics are all mythological and unworkable. The unrealistic expectation is that the righteous are divinely rewarded and the wicked justly punished.

The primary aim of Intelligent Morality is to develop and equip people with the tested and proven knowledge and skills which will enable them to achieve their Good goals and the ability to determine what is Good in the long and lasting term as well as to recognize who and what actually produces Evil—including those beliefs and persons sincerely and devoutly intending to do Good, but actually producing Evil through their foolishness, ineptitude, incompetence, lack of ability and knowledge, poor training or reliance on falsehoods and bad practices, even those sanctioned by the religions, professions, governments and academia.

Whereas Revealed Religion creates the illusion that Good intentions and religious beliefs alone are enough to produce Good results because the Gods have supposedly designed reality to function in this way and intervene to assist those with Good intentions, Intelligent Morality makes no such demonstrably false assumptions and instead gathers and collates data and knowledge, tests hypotheses and experiments to determine the actual results, as opposed to purely logical conclusions and religious dogmas, and shares this acquired and accumulated knowledge with those in need when it is moral to do so—meaning it does NOT help enemies of the group to harm the group or individual or advance their hostile cause.

Some believe that absolute standards of morality in the form of supposedly divinely Revealed Religion are inherently superior to individual or group moral codes, judgements or decisions as to what constitutes Good or Evil in the real world and supposed supernatural realm, if only because they set a universal standard to follow even if they are not in truth divinely inspired and revealed. If it is presumed that an absolute and loving God says it is Evil to murder and steal, that is an inherently better standard to universally follow than allowing for an individual to make alternative determinations of what constitutes Good and Evil, which permits an individual person to believe and assert that it is instead Good to murder and steal.

But what if the Revealed Religion's dogma asserts that it is Good to murder and steal as in the case of the Old Testament? Who can oppose that false belief other than the Intelligently Moral? Revealed Religion is the danger, not Intelligent Morality which enables anyone to oppose any belief no matter who holds it whether the alleged believers in Evil are psychopaths, religious people or Intelligently Moral. Just because one person or group says that something is moral or immoral does not mean that anyone else has to agree with them, cannot oppose them, or that they will change their mind just because a Revealed Religion tells them they ought to.

Advocates of this argument usually neglect to mention the fact that many religions command and compel not only murder and theft, but complete genocide as well (for example *Deuteronomy* chapters 7, 20 and 25. I *Samuel* 15). In this regard, Revealed Religion is proven to have incited murder, theft and genocide. Intelligent Morality affords the individual and group the opportunity to assess such religious commandments and reject them as being a shock to the conscience, an offense to reason and experience, immoral and Evil, or simply impractical and inefficacious.

The religious, on the other hand, believe they have no choice but to obey these divine commandments which shock their conscience and contradict experience. They believe that they are compelled to have faith and obey the Gods even in instances where their religion compels them to murder, steal and commit genocide as part of the supposedly divine plan. Intelligent Morality is clearly more moral than such religions based on the assertion that murder, theft and genocide are inherently and obviously Evil to most.

The existence of a Revealed Religion which asserts that it is Evil to murder and steal does not prevent anyone from believing that it is instead Good to murder and steal. Therefore the religious standard is in no sense absolute or universal. If one person believes it is instead Good to murder and steal in spite of the religious dogma, that does not compel anyone else to agree. There is no practical difference between disagreements between religious beliefs and non-religious beliefs, and those within and among non-religious beliefs, other than dogmatically. Appeal to dogmatic authority has no necessary effect on what a person actually believes in their private thoughts or does, and often provokes unspoken reflexive rebellion against it. The dogmatic standards of various and often contradictory religions can as easily be accepted or rejected by anyone as any personal or general standard which the believer admits to be of purely human origin, and therefore religions bear no advantage other than to the priest class and the self-righteous who assert that they have divine authority.

Though some feel compelled to follow religious standards out of fear, their Will often overcomes their fear. In many instances it is more effective to convince a person that it is in their own best interest to act according to a given moral code and to demonstrate to them the tested fact with sound evidence, reasonable explanations and relatable examples.

It is fallacious to assert that Revealed Religion produces actual absolute universal standards. There are many religions with differing definitions of Good and Evil and therefore many conflicting and contradictory standards of what is Revealed Religion and what is not. Among those varying Revealed Religions, each society, group, family and individual uniquely interprets what are fallaciously called "universal and absolute" moral standards, but are in practice universal and absolute in name only.

Every person must of necessity assess how these arbitrarily set standards are applied in every varying circumstance in their lives in ways in which others may disagree based upon the same dogmatic set of rules and like conditions. Even the translation of these rules from one language and era to another introduces different interpretations of what the Gods supposedly said, intended, taught and demand. There is no absoluteness or universality to any Revealed Religion. Religion is always understood and applied in unique and *relative* ways by unique individuals under differing circumstances.

The specific examples of murder and theft as being instinctively and intuitively Evil *per se* due to the observable harm they cause innocent people and the shock and horror they cause the conscience is often irrationally generalized to demonstrate the alleged superiority of Revealed Religions which proscribe murder and theft, because they serve as a standard that prevents individuals from asserting otherwise that murder and theft are instead supposedly Good. As was shown, this is a fallacy of false generalization, because in fact many Revealed Religions encourage and command rape, slavery, murder and theft, and other specific examples can be cited which evince the instinctive and intuitive superiority of Intelligent Morality over Revealed Religion, as in the case of the New Testament where Jesus Christ and Paul broke with their God's laws by working for food and healing the sick on the Sabbath Day and by not compelling the Gentiles to be circumcised in order to receive the Covenant. In these instances, Jesus and Paul were practicing Intelligent Morality in the guise of Revealed Religion and demonstrated that reason trumps faith. Modern moral codes generally condemn the genocide, rape, theft, murder and slavery that the Old Testament frequently commands and compels.

The presumption of the superiority of Revealed Religion based upon carefully chosen specific examples is a fallacy of false generalization and contradicted by other known examples. The determination of superiority between Revealed Religion and Intelligent Morality is therefore not based upon the supposedly divine nature of the revelation, as opposed to an individual's informed and rational choice, but rather on the expected and experienced outcomes and individual conscience, or lack thereof, of the person arriving at their judgement of whether or not specific conduct or beliefs are inherently Good or Evil. Revealed Religion holds no edge and many disadvantages in this contest because it prevents its adherents from objecting to obviously Evil standards which the Intelligently Moral are free to oppose no matter who alleges that Evil beliefs and acts are instead Good.

In fact, only individual morality can oppose a proposed or accepted universal standard which asserts that murder, theft or genocide are moral, because only an individual or group can declare that the tenets of a Revealed Religion are false. If a Revealed Religion states instead that murder and theft are Good, as many do, then it is considered the crime of blasphemy to disagree and call murder and theft Evil. If, on the other hand, an individual asserts that it is Intelligently Moral to murder and steal, as some do, then others are free to publicly disagree, condemn and criticize that belief which shocks their conscience, horrifies them and contradicts their experience. They are free to seek legal prohibitions against such conduct and punishment for such acts. Therefore, Intelligent Morality is inherently superior to Revealed Religion because it is not subject to the charge of blasphemy and is NOT dogmatically authoritative compelling Evil acts and thoughts, and only those who are Intelligently Moral can decry the false morality of Revealed Religions which assert that murder, theft and genocide are Good. The devoutly religious cannot oppose their own horrific beliefs.

The generalized assertion that an individual or group practicing Intelligent Morality is always more prone to Evil than the religious community is demonstrably false and the tacit presumption that Revealed Religion is always instinctively and intuitively Good is also a proven falsehood. Deciding whether a given pair of examples between Intelligent Morality and Revealed Religion exhibit the superiority of one system over the other is often both an objective and a subjective matter, which in itself demonstrates the superiority of the inherent flexibility and adaptability of Intelligent Morality, which openly allows for and compels this assessment, which of necessity also occurs in every practical application of Revealed Religion which must also of necessity incorporate differing understandings and interpretations of religious dogma in its application to varying circumstances and persons, unique interpretations which are complex and of necessity vary between persons and groups. The difference is that the Intelligently Moral pursue this assessment in a purely realistic and tested manner which questions dogma instead of relying upon it and the religious act on faith alone.

Religiously inclined people sometimes assert that human beings cannot create just moral codes because of their conflict of interest in placing their own self-interests above those of others. This tacitly and falsely presumes the unproven and irrational conclusion that self-interest is unjust and inherently immoral. The incentive certainly exists to skew morality to favor one's own personal profile, benefit and agenda, but there is nothing inherently Evil or unjust in that. Morality exists to benefit the individual and group and is fulfilling its purpose when it does so. It does not exist in reality to please the Gods. Interests often do conflict and what is just must be determined based upon the fact that the individual acting is doing so in his or her own best interest and that is NOT inherently Evil or unjust.

As an historical example, heterosexuals will favor heterosexuality, as will an unsubverted society in general because it is procreative and perpetuates the tribe and race, while homosexuals demand their right to be themselves and preserve their human dignity while following their innate desires and nature. But it is this very fact that interests can and often do conflict which makes the ability to determine for one's self what is moral and just the superior benefit of Intelligent Morality, because it enables an individual to judge for him or herself what is Moral, Good and Evil and to pursue greater knowledge to obtain more efficacious and successful means to improve their lives and the lives of others, rather than relying on the assumption that the Gods will favor or oppose their behavior based on its conformity or disobedience to the arbitrary laws and dogmatic decrees the Gods supposedly communicated to human beings, which may or may not best serve them.

Knowledge trumps faith. The person whose innate nature

is justified and viewed as Good by his or her moral code is acting in a rational and justifiable manner to thrive and survive, but that does not prevent conflicts with others, nothing does, even surrendering one's best interests to another. The conflict remains in such a case, but one side has chosen to capitulate rather than fight, and that, too, is immoral and Evil.

An immigrant or invader into another country may logically determine and scientifically demonstrate that immigration or invasion is morally Good and Just, and benefits his or her survival and the perpetuation of his or her kind and descendants. A native in that country may concurrently logically and scientifically determine that immigration or invasion is Evil, Unjust and detrimental to his or her survival and the perpetuation of his or her kind and like descendants. It is irrational to assert that everyone is best served by a general universal moral standard, and that because one moral standard conflicts with another, one standard must be chosen to become a singular universal standard over all others among all humanity. That would represent defeat and capitulation by some to the benefit of others, often through subterfuge, deceit and violence, not innate moral superiority.

It is instead rational to conclude that different moral standards best serve different people and groups and they are foolish to not abide their own best interests and are unjust to themselves if they fail to do so. Every person has a different appearance. Every person has a right to their own morality and standard of justice. Conflicts exist and imposing a standard that is scientifically shown to be Moral and Just for one person, but which is Unjust and Immoral to another with a conflicting interest is irrational. Instead, one will often prevail over the other and the same outcome will be Good for one and Evil for the other. Morality is not universal or absolute. Intelligent Morality is superior to Revealed Religion because it acknowledges this demonstrated fact and enables individuals and groups to defend their own best interests from their enemies and competitors.

People can and most often do have conflicting and opposing interests. The highest morality is survival and survival of self and kind is the priority among competing interests and people. It is NOT of necessity immoral to pursue survival and those who do not ensure their own survival, and the survival of their kind, demonstrably harm themselves and their own kind and often cease to exist, which is quintessentially Evil for them.

The implicit determination that it is better to have one universal standard as the common moral currency has in its favor the notion that it is better to have one moral code than many because only then can everyone know what is officially taken to be Immoral and what is Moral and apply those set standards to everyone equally. But this rests on the false assumptions that everyone will be familiar with these set standards and that they will agree with and to them and abide by them; and that having a single code of what is morally proscribed and permitted is necessarily the most beneficial circumstance for individuals and their unique societies at large, and for the majority without imposing the tyranny of the majority on minorities.

It makes no difference that one moral standard is spuriously called "absolute and universal" in name but in name only, when in practice the majority of people either do not understand the supposedly, though in name only, absolute and universal morality, interpret it differently, or reject it outright in favor of something else. Each person must of necessity come to an individual and ever changing understanding of morality which will differ from all others due to their unique nature and experience and must of necessity apply it in unique ways to different and often unforeseen circumstances.

The survival of society is contingent upon the survival of its members. Different members better their chances of survival with different moral codes due to their different interests, nature and circumstances. It is also a false and arbitrary assumption to assert that the survival of every society is a better moral outcome than the survival of certain individuals or groups at the expense of others. There are often enmities and conflicting interests between individuals and groups and each must determine what is Good for them. Just because something is Good for one person or group does not mean it is Good for everyone alive on the face of the Earth. Revealed Religion can and often does conflict with what is Good for an individual or group and is therefore Evil for them, if not also for everyone, as is demonstrably the case in apocalyptic religions which compel the extermination of humanity to cleanse the Earth of it which is the worst Evil imaginable (*Zephaniah* 1).

The abstract notion of the universality of Revealed Religion is a delusion that presumes and fosters the unrealistic, counterproductive and inhibiting presumption of a nonexistent divine judge who theoretically can and sometimes will intervene to assist those who obey it in the pursuit of Good and punish and hinder those who do not and instead deliberately pursue what has supposedly been deemed Evil by an omnipresent, omnipotent and omniscient being. It also presumes that every person is capable of understanding the dogmas presented to them as if Revealed Religion, which is certainly not the case. In fact, many

Christians believe they must commune with the Holy Spirit to properly understand their confusing and sometimes self-contradictory dogmas, and let God into their hearts to determine spiritually for them what their unaided heads cannot reason out because the dogma itself is irrational, self-destructive and internally inconsistent on its face (*John* 16:12-15. I *Corinthians* 2:14).

The presumption that Revealed Religion comes from Gods is false. Human beings created and create it. Given that humans create Revealed Religion, they are no less capable and competent to create and evolve Intelligent Morality. People are just as able to create moral codes as they are to create laws and the creation of just laws is an even greater responsibility than the creation of moral codes because the full force of the violent State imposes and enforces the Law sometimes upon pain of death.

In reality, absolute standards suffer the defect of being immutable and therefore unadaptable as general guides, which defect is often asserted as if it were divinely Revealed Religion's greatest virtue. Absolute standards are also inherently limited after having been set in stone forever and are absurd when they contradict each other. They can often only be applied as an analogue without specificity to a given set of forever changing circumstances and human beings are obliged to determine for themselves how to apply obsolete standards to changing circumstances making people the arbiters and creators of moral standards through their own interpretations, not the imaginary Gods. The absolute immutability and inflexibility of Revealed Religion even in the face of overwhelmingly contradictory evidence is potentially a fatal flaw, one which has brought down entire civilizations such as the Aztecs who welcomed in their conquerors due to the Aztecs' supposedly revealed divine prophecy that the White Men coming to kill them were instead benevolent Gods.

Absolute divinely inspired morality implies that those who intend to do Good as defined dogmatically by their religion will be assisted in this pursuit by divine forces which will help them to achieve Good. Their faith in divine intervention and providence often results in delusions, complacency and laziness, and substitutes faith for action, study, thought and the collection, collation and realistic assessment of data under the highest current standards of logic and reason. The untested belief that Revealed Religion is absolutely true is a fatal flaw. Intelligent Morality asserts logical standards based on known empirical facts. It is skeptical of its own assertions and continually tests them and creates new hypotheses.

The belief in absolute divinely inspired morality also implies that those intending to do Evil will be assisted by supernatural Evil Forces and opposed by supernatural Good Forces. This leads many to surrender their control over their own fate to nonexistent imaginary beings and to fail to take appropriate measures to determine the best course of action based on facts, data and logic. It is better to rely upon tested knowledge than faith. It is better to seize control over one's fate than to fatalistically pretend that everything is in God's hands and will follow God's plan regardless of what we do or don't do, and therefore we need not or dare not do anything. The religiously inclined often blame the victim of a tragedy for their fate because they assume the pain they suffer is somehow divine punishment.

All of these delusions create a self-defeating mythology that is also self-justifying because when Revealed Religion fails to produce the intended results its followers seek they unrealistically attribute their failure to Divine Will or

Satanic Forces, not the failure of the person or group to properly comprehend, assess and address the situation in a productive, original, adaptive, creative and beneficial manner that produces a predictable Good outcome with reasonable certainty. Those who subject themselves to revealed religious beliefs see the World as they think it ought to be based on fictitious arbitrary standards and dogmas, rather than as it measurably and actually is, and are therefore often unable to alter the course of events in the most effective and beneficial ways to produce the most Good.

Relying on a belief in divine justice, often supposedly imposed postmortem in heaven or hell, contributes to ignorance and the perpetuation of practices which generate Evil results again and again without fail as in the case of circumcision and the denigration and abuse of children and women. Those who commit atrocious acts often go unpunished because they intended to do Good or relied on religious dogma, but failed miserably due to their mistakes, ignorance, negligence, false beliefs, unwillingness to learn and reassess, failure to gather and assess data, lack of proper knowledge, etc.

Divinely inspired morality often serves as justification and an excuse to do Evil, or do nothing, by the failure to take the necessary and frequently cumbersome and expensive steps which increase the probability of achieving Good. Reliance is placed on the faith that the Gods will not allow those intending to do Good to fail even though they fail to do what is necessary to increase their scientifically determined probability of success. The non-religious are equally prone to be negligent and incompetent if they fail to abide by their moral requirement to become informed, trained and knowledgeable. For example many doctors are incompetent and do tremendous harm to their patients despite their Good intentions. The same is true of many parents who unintentionally do terribly Evil things to their kids falsely believing what they do is Good.

A scientifically based system of morality is infinitely superior to supposed divinely Revealed Religion in that it of necessity increases the probability of Good versus Evil outcomes, because it compiles and assesses data, falsifies falsehoods and informs us as to what has been successfully tested in the past under like conditions and what has not. Science achieves this end by applying logic to acquired facts and testing hypotheses instead of presuming unproven results based on supposition, logic alone or authoritative dogma. Science does not rely upon divine or supernatural Good and Evil Forces to obtain predictable and desirable outcomes, nor does it depend upon Metaphysics or logic alone. Instead, it accumulates data-driven tested knowledge and classifies it non-dogmatically as the logical assessment of a certain set of data at a given time in a specified set of circumstances, based upon the tested empirical observation that like conditions produce like results. A laymen with access to Artificial Intelligence that correctly assesses and diagnoses a person's ailment produces Good through knowledge, while an incompetent or deluded doctor who improperly diagnoses and/or mistreats a patient commits a terrible act of Evil often with the best of intentions. Intentions are not enough. Knowledge, ideas, training, tools, data, measurements, etc. are often needed. Knowing the tricks of the trade is far more useful than prayer or faith.

Science does not presume that Good supernatural forces will intervene when a person intends to do Good or Evil, but instead provides the unbiased knowledge and tools needed to assist an individual, group, society or mankind to anticipate the results of choices and behaviors. Revealed Religion relies upon the test of time to either result in catastrophe or survival and is only adaptable if the priest class, prophets, lunatics or charlatans claim that the Gods have spoken to them and revealed new or different standards of morality, as in the case of Christianity's Jesus and Paul.

On the other hand, Christianity absurdly claims that it is moral to love one's enemies and turn the other cheek in the pursuit of earning supposed immortality. Intelligent Morality recognizes that enemies are living organisms which exist in the physical world and that our perceptions and interpretations of these enemies are abstractions which can and often do contribute to our own destruction, especially if we adopt such deliberately subversive religious mythologies as Christianity's dogmatic insistence on loving enemies, putting the enemy's interests first and tolerating the enemy's abuse.

It is not only possible, but absolutely necessary to have two or more different intellectual and emotional approaches to the same physical object and task. There are different ways of viewing, perceiving, conceptualizing and treating the very same physical entities and beings for entirely different purposes. We can look upon a painting as a beloved work of art and experience and appreciate it aesthetically and emotionally as it hangs motionless on the wall versus the totally different perception of the same painting we adopt when moving it from point A to point B, which is a physical problem and task in the real world that correctly objectifies the painting as a mass that must be moved, not an abstract source of pleasure and contemplation in our consciousness.

Mortal enemies must be perceived in the same manner as any other physical challenge that must be overcome and defeated in the real world if we are to survive and thrive in the biological confrontation that will determine whose DNA will survive. Intelligent Morality is the morality of survival.

We have to view mortal enemies as biological competitors for existence and assess their physical characteristics and how to defeat the threat that they pose to us in the real world and not play some abstract mental game trying to see ourselves in them and view things from their hostile vantage point which denigrates us. It is Good to preserve oneself and one's kind. Intelligent Morality compels us to defeat our enemies in the real world and win the physical, biological competition, not love them or allow them to harm us in the vain hope of achieving immortality and postmortem rewards which are never actually bestowed upon the duped martyr. Our defense against our enemies must be practical and physically real involving physical and biological processes which defend us and defeat them. We have to treat the situation as a physical and biological problem that requires physical and biological solutions. Survival is morally Good.

Human beings are relatively frail animals and that weakness of our enemy can be exploited and compels us to wage an intelligent as well as physical response to their attack and plans to destroy us. Since our enemy plans to enslave and exterminate the weak and stupid among us and themselves bear exploitable flaws known to me, we can leapfrog over our enemy and eugenically improve our kind.

We should view our defense against our enemies not as a war between nonexistent supernatural forces of Good versus Evil, but instead realistically determine that our survival is Good and the success of our enemy would be Evil because it would annihilate us. It is not necessary to morally justify our defense beyond this fact. We should not view the enemy religiously, abstractly, spiritually or universally, nor mistakenly assume that supernatural forces are at work and at our disposal, or that our enemy should be viewed abstractly in terms of their souls, rights, good qualities, etc. as opposed to their real physical presence as biological organisms and threats in the real physical world who seek our absolute destruction.

Survival of the fittest means that we must alter our environment to make it fit for our survival and unfit for our enemies. One aspect of making the environment fit for our survival is to extract or quarantine the fifth column and Trojan horse the enemy has implanted among us. It is also vital to remove all the physical and mental weapons the enemy uses against us and which they have implanted in our physical and mental environment. Beyond that, we must also creatively adapt our physical and mental environment to make it conducive in general to our survival and the continuation of life on Earth. We must survive the misrule of our puppet leaders who are working for our enemies to take away our lives and erase our DNA from existence.

Our goal is to perpetuate our own kind, not to go extinct or evolve into something else due to a changing environment in which we are unfit to survive. We should not seek to adapt our organism to a changed world and thereby exterminate our own kind, but instead maintain a fit world and when necessary change the world to render it a suitably healthy and safe place in which to live and produce children.

Revealed Religion often stands in the way of these pursuits. Intelligent Morality does not, it creates awareness of, fosters and compels them.

Chapter Three
Free Will and Dogmatism

Truly Free Will cannot be driven by fear of damnation, faithful adherence to religious dogma, the duress and coercion of peer pressure or Church politics—nor is it the product of indoctrination. It can be achieved to varying degrees by the logical interpretation of facts and application of knowledge if the potential opportunities sought already exist, are possible or can be created. Good and Evil do not create or inhibit Free Will. They are instead a subjective and abstract assessment of facts and causality not inherent in the physical world itself.

Children are more apt to exercise their will in productive and Good ways if they are shown and convinced of what is Good, why it is Good and how it will help them and those they love, than if they are intimidated or traumatized into accepting a belief. Fear and trauma are in themselves often destructive and generate reflexes, neuroses and compulsions, rather than a Free Will. Children respond better to realistic education which makes them aware of what will benefit them and what can harm them, than to fear of the bogeyman of damnation in the dark and fiery closet of Hell.

Free Will without temperance, sound knowledge and insightful wisdom is apt to produce Evil in many cases. Pornography, promiscuity and other issues related to the normal and natural sex drive are frequently destructive to otherwise healthy relationships and marriages. The knowledge of what promotes the health of Good relationships and what tends to destroy them is incredibly useful in fulfilling the Free Will's desire for a long, healthy and happy coexistence with a mate and a family.

False knowledge can be worse than ignorance, as can bad advice or incompetent work done by professionals and trades people. Withholding facts, data, the tested truth and skeptical criticism frequently inhibits the Free action of the Will to attain Good. Enemies often deliberately offer knowingly bad advice. Politicians deliberately misrepresent the facts and best interests of the People. Professionals frequently fail to study their own fields of expertise to the extent needed to offer the best service possible to their clients. Professions often betray their ethical, moral and scientific principles and instead rely upon obsolete, false, disproven and authoritative dogmas. They also frequently fail to collect and properly assess data, act without preconceived bias, follow their own best standards, or engage in experimentation, theorization or shared information.

If there were truly Free Will and the Gods existed, then the Gods would ensure that those with Good intentions produced Good results as the result of their Free Will having intended to do so. Will which cannot achieve its goals is NOT Free, it is an illusion, frustration and often a detriment. The supposedly Free Will of a religious person who wishes to do Good, but instead creates Evil outcomes, has NOT enjoyed any sort of freedom, other than the choice to intend to do Good which has instead yielded Evil, Evil that sometimes further restricts the person and which may even kill the person or his or her loved ones—potentially hundreds of millions or even billions of people.

Freer Will, that is *effective* Will can be attained by learning the tricks of the trade and the skills and opportunities needed to create, repair or change things which the ignorant, unskilled, inept and otherwise ineffective person cannot. Revealed Religion does not provide a sound basis for determining what is actually Good in practice, as opposed to theory, or how to achieve it. Revealed Religion instead creates the false expectation that intent is enough to succeed, which complacent delusion often prevents those intending to do Good from taking the necessary steps to actually achieve the results they seek or something even better than they initially anticipated, because they falsely believe they need do no more than have faith and mean well.

Knowledge can provide the power to do Good which truly frees the Will to do so. Intelligent Morality is a superior means of obtaining and developing that necessary knowledge. Intelligent Morality also tests the often unproven expectation of the Will that something it desires is actually Good, though it may not be.

To a greater extent in the past and still in many societies, parents would help to arrange marriages for their children. Their experience, knowledge and awareness of cultural and traditional norms, mores and beliefs helped guide them to produce Good outcomes and perpetuate tested lifestyles. The supposedly Free Will to find a fitting and successful spouse does not of itself guarantee either the opportunity for, or success of any given match or type of match. Parental or other advice based on tested experience and knowledge passed down for thousands of years is often helpful in making a successful match. That would be an example of applied Intelligent Morality as opposed to blind faith in Free Will with the intent to do Good but not the tools to achieve it.

Bad advice, impulsiveness, failure to realistically assess a person, allowing emotion and feelings to triumph over reason, desperation, etc. can lead a person to enter into and sustain a bad and harmful relationship. A bad marriage can be an Evil and terribly costly tragedy in a person's life and is often entered into with the best of intentions; but without sufficient data, experience, standards, criteria, critical thought or patience needed to increase the likelihood of success that may increase with *proper* parental or other advice.

On the other hand, *improper* advice from friends or fools can result in catastrophe. Gods which do not exist cannot intervene to prevent or correct this. Intelligent Morality encourages a realistic approach to freeing the Will to achieve beneficial, lasting and Good results. It also dismisses a dogmatic or religious acceptance of maxims, tenets, doctrines and beliefs which are untested or factually contradicted by experience or logic.

Chapter Four
Politics, Mass Manipulation and Group Behavior

Revealed Religion plays a major role in politics and is a very effective means of manipulating group behavior and controlling and subjugating the masses. Religious figures often assert dogmatic moral superiority and authority which supposedly cannot be questioned. They short circuit critical thinking by merely alleging that they are Christians, and somehow therefore righteous and capable of understanding things others are not.

Religious demagogues frequently try to foment an "us against them" polarized group mentality and deliberately portray themselves as shepherds leading a flock of obedient sheep who follow God and need fear being led astray by agents of Satan. They pretend to have the force of the Gods behind them and rebuke people in the name of their Gods instead of engaging in rational discourse, often because they know they will lose an argument and therefore appeal to the emotions and feelings of their audience rather than to their reason.

People are susceptible to the propaganda of demagogues because of the peer pressure of the mob who attempt to mimic the figurehead and leader and silence and punish anyone who questions their authority figure. Religious leaders and comedians make especially effective propagandists because their audience becomes engrossed in the uncritical emotional religious or comedic experience, singing and laughter. They turn and look at one another in nodding approval to further enjoy the shared experience of the group which is scripted and directed by its leader. Anyone who questions the dogma or opinions the propagandist is promoting is immediately branded as an enemy of the group, crazy and dangerous—even satanic.

All a subversive agent need do to win the support of the religious group for the subversive agenda he or she is advancing, is to become a member of the religious group and speak in its name. The agenda of the subversive *agents provocateur* then becomes the agenda of the entire religion and its followers. A prearranged claque is often present at such performances to cheer on the speaker and mislead the rest of the audience to believe there is a popular and general acceptance of what is being said even if it obscenely violates the standards of the community up to that point.

Such people usually promote an Evil and subversive agenda and try to make it taboo to expose what they are doing as they coopt the religion or political movement. They conceal and distort facts needed to properly assess a situation. They lie and promote the enemies of the group as if their saviors. They lead their flock into mousetraps. Many are charismatic psychopaths who use their charm to gain the group's trust and admiration based on personal appeal rather than actual character and substance. The enchanted group then becomes ensnared and defends them against all others even those who are legitimately trying to saving them from their enemy.

Advertising often works in much the same way. The tobacco lobby employed the most corrupt means to obstruct the public's awareness of the deadly risks of tobacco use. They refuted scientifically determined facts. They commissioned and paid for alternative studies which misrepresented the dangers of tobacco. Tobacco companies created labels and images which appealed to children, the subconscious and the emotions. Hollywood worked together with the liquor and tobacco industries to promote the internal consumption of addictive poisons.

Intelligent Morality elevates the culture and standards of society in order to reduce the gullibility and susceptibility of the masses to corruption. A properly educated populace of people who are intellectually advanced enough to demand reasoned discourse and exposure of the facts is more apt to produce Good. They are also better suited to be productive members of society and produce a safer, more civilized environment in which to live. An ignorant and deluded populace is more susceptible to Evil agents and agendas, including self-destructive agendas.

The existence of a sound social system, government, training, educational agenda, economy, etc. is not enough. The culture, beliefs, genetic nature, intellectual and physical abilities, traditions, standards, etc. of the people are even more important to the success of a society and its ability to do Good for its members then the Constitution and leadership of the nation. There are peoples which are incapable of taking advantage of the benefits of an entire social environment which functions quite well for a different set and type of people. There are also people who can make a system that fails others function for them, even though they inherently prefer a better system of their own making and historic habit and are only forced to live in the inferior and inhibited system created by people unlike them. Cultural norms, mores and standards affect the efficacy of moral codes and what works for the benefit of both the majority and minority in one society will not of necessity be effective for an entirely different society.

Our enemy realizes that we seek a political system which betters our lives and recognize some of the defects in the present system and society in general. The enemy dupes the masses into adopting false Utopian beliefs in politics just as it has in supposedly Revealed Religions. Marxism, open borders and many other subversive and destructive political movements stem from the enemy who knows in advance that they will be harmful, but sells them to the public as if they were Utopian panaceas. They often provoke the masses to destroy their own nations and governments in the vain hopes of creating a Utopia, often a global Utopia.

The enemy has tricked many societies into destroying their own institutions and economies with the best intentions in ways that led to the worst Evil humanity has ever suffered as in the case of Marxism. Marxism is another instance, like the Revealed Religion Christianity, where people are taught that their Good intentions are enough to produce Good outcomes, but when tried and tested, instead cause the worst Evil in history.

Marxism is still promoted as if it were created with Good intentions and produces Good outcomes, when the facts of history reveal how genocidal, dysgenic, destructive of liberty and fratricidal it intentionally is and always was. Marxists and the enemy attempt to suppress these facts and restrict this knowledge. Marxists are intensely dogmatic. Intelligent Morality recognizes that it is immoral to be dogmatic, because dogmatic authority often perpetuates Evil and compels Evil acts, and it frequently prohibits Good and Good actions.

Political systems tend to be inherently authoritarian and dogmatic given the nature of the State and its powers. For this reason and many others, they tend to be dysgenic and self-destructive over time. Even the best societies are corrupted to become Evil and degenerate. Properly documenting and assessing history is a very useful method for Intelligent Morality, which our enemy always attempts to subvert and prohibit.

History affords us with many examples of different ways to establish an independent sovereign State. A new political and media class can be nurtured and overtake a government. Large numbers of likeminded people can move to a territory and then secede or use their combined influence to obtain independence. A minority population can declare that the oppression it suffers justifies its formation of a new country. A majority population can recognize that it has been subverted and clean its house of the adversary.

An Intelligently Moral society must develop and maintain military advantages over its adversaries. Our enemy will seek to pit the world against us. It will be necessary to counter their lies through diplomatic methods to regulate foreign public opinion and prevent their espionage and subversion. It will also be necessary to present a credible deterrence to their aggression.

The internet provides us with a means to affect public opinion around the world. Artificial Intelligence enables us to collect data and assess trigger words, memes and methods of controlling the public discourse and public opinion. The enemy uses these means to terrible effect and we can just as easily employ them to our benefit. We will also identify and track our enemies, keep databases of who they are and how their networks are interconnected, and focus our countermeasures on those who pose the greatest threat so as to maximize the effect of our defenses.

As the enemy drags down the rest of humanity, we will gain many competitive advantages simply by sustaining ourselves. As we advance, and they decline, the gap will grow even larger in our favor. A eugenically inclined society is inherently more likely to survive and improve than one in which all its institutions are engineered to reduce the quality of its members and make them more controllable and internally powerless.

Our ancestors were aware of most of this and responsibly treated foreign threats and hostile subversive groups and movements as an enemy to be disposed of and eliminated. Instead of abstractly attempting to emotionally respond to the feelings and rights of the enemy from its hostile perspective, they treated it as a physical threat, defeated and expelled it.

Both Intelligent Morality and Revealed Religion are susceptible to deceit and manipulation by people and powers intent on doing harm or taking advantage of others. Both can lead to a false sense of security and submission to hostile, unethical or mistaken authority. The gullible, trusting, uninformed, unintelligent, desperate, disadvantaged, targeted and inept are easy prey to those out to harm them or take advantage of them.

Both scientists and religious zealots can presume to be morally superior, holier than thou and possess an unquestionable and irrefutable truth that dare not be doubted or questioned. Both are used to persuade people to do and allow things which are against their own best interests, often in the name of morality. But when doubts and questions do arise, Intelligent Morality affords the opportunity to present the data, facts and logical assessment needed to act with the highest probability of success if, and only if, its tenets are freely and fully followed.

Politics, politicians, the press and religion all have a tremendous impact on people's lives. They can accomplish great Good or inflict terrible Harm. Wealth disparity, unequal treatment and governmental and media access of different groups and individuals severely impacts the quality of life, life span and success of different members of a society and their offspring and kind.

The few often rule over and manipulate the masses by controlling and manufacturing public opinion in many ways. Though they bear and pretend to honor a fiduciary responsibility to their subjects, serfs and slaves, they also maintain a conflict of interest and place their own perceived self and group interests above those of the masses they govern and control. Rulers often lie, withhold vital information and deliberately or accidentally cause horrific harm to those whom they rule. Leaders have an incentive to oppress and hinder the masses they lead in order to prevent any competition for their power and control. Accumulated wealth does not equate to superior genes, intellect, ability or other qualities. Quite often the best genetic material is found in the lower classes. Many societies tend to prevent the best people from rising and instead promote parasites, psychopaths, sycophants, cowards and thieves who depend upon the talents and superior genetics of the people they oppress and exploit for their financial and political success.

Intelligent Morality compels people to be competent at their jobs, whether it be as police, politicians, bankers, teachers, parents, etc. A society with high competency but low rates of belief in Revealed Religion will produce a better quality of life, greater Good and less Evil than a society with high Revealed Religion but low competency levels. There are many historical examples of this and it serves as evidence that the Gods do not intervene on behalf of believers and that Science yields more productive results and has greater efficacy than Faith if put to Good purposes with sound methodology. Science is therefore potentially more Moral than Faith alone. Though there is not a necessary mutual exclusion between Faith and Science, there can be contradictory standards; just as there can between various Faiths and differing scientific conclusions; as there always is between groups with conflicting and opposing interests. It is not the purpose of Intelligent Morality to become arrogant, self-satisfied, complacent, negligent, dogmatic, authoritative or lax.

There is a marked and preferable distinction between Morality and Law in an Intelligently Moral society. Laws must be absolute and universal standards among the groups to which they apply. There can certainly be laws which apply to some and not others, as for example laws regarding citizens and non-citizens and their rights and privileges as in the case of voting rights. The relative nature of Intellectual Morality which is its inherent strength is maintained in the Law through the assertion of relative defenses and just reasons for violating the absolute standards of the Law, which must to the greatest degree possible inform the public as to what is permitted and what is proscribed lest the Law be too vague to be understood or enforceable. This is a sophisticated and complex set of concepts best left to internal future discussion.

Our enemy uses our governmentally protected freedoms to take away our freedom by acting collectively and collusively to monopolize and privatize every avenue of public and private life and remove our governmental protections by asserting their private rights. This is quite obvious in the public arena of Free Speech where the enemy uses the First Amendment protection of Free Speech in the public forums it monopolizes through wealth to curtail the Free Speech of the majority by censoring and barring anyone who expresses speech the monopolistic owners seek to silence and suppress. The solution is to extend the governmental protection of rights to private institutions and to remove enemies from society who deliberately take advantage of our freedoms to deprive us of our freedoms.

There are people and groups who are incompatible with a free society and who must be excluded from free societies. We recognize this fact with regard to violent offenders who physically attack us, but fail to apply the same principle to those who commit violence against our fundamental rights. That has to end. Freedoms which can be violated by private parties so as to make them the unelected governors of our lives are freedoms in name only which are selectively granted to the few so that they can impose their tyranny on the many.

Changes, reforms and defensive actions often need to be comprehensive in order to be effective. It is not enough to mandate a healthy diet in school lunches if the farmers and ranchers are concurrently barred from producing healthy food. It is not enough to guarantee Free Speech to all on the Federal Governmental level if private institutions which monopolize and control the public square that influences politics and public opinion do not permit Free Speech to all on a level and fair playing field. Libertarianism is a crypto-Communist movement which seeks to destroy the US dollar and replace it with private currencies that can function with a social credit system like in Communist China. Libertarians call for the functions of government to be privatized so that the wealthy can monopolize them and impose their tyranny on the public without the masses having any recourse to their Federal rights, privileges and protections. They seek to enslave us in the private tyranny of Plutocracy in the name of liberating us from the government.

We cannot have a free society when disproportionately influential people seek out every opportunity to enslave and exterminate us. Freedoms must be accompanied by education, culture, patriotism, cohesiveness and a common sense of purpose, or they will be exploited to produce ruin and oppression.

Solutions must be multifaceted and comprehensive in order to be effective. Providing weapons to an ally in their battle against an aggressor is not an effective solution if you concurrently make it impossible for your ally to use them. Having modern hospitals is not a guarantee of good health care and a healthy population. Well trained physicians are also necessary, as is a public who look after their own health, as is an immigration system and leadership who keep immigrants with contagious diseases out of the country. Solutions must be multifaceted and comprehensive in order to be effective.

One of the benefits of a homogenous and unified nation is that there are fewer variables. Diversity is not always a strength. A person pointing a gun at you because he views you as different from him and vulnerable is not an advantage to you. Uniformity and regularity increase the probability of accurate forecasts and eases the interpretation and application of data. A uniformly moral, intelligent and normal society is an infinitely better place to live in than an atomized, chaotic and criminal world.

Chapter Five
Prayer and Action

Knowledge and action are far more effective agents to bring about Good and prevent Evil than prayer, talismans, magical charms like crucifixes, blessings from a priest, reciting passages from a holy book, etc. Praying for manna from heaven is not a viable alternative to working the soil and planting crops.

Instincts and innate drives which are inhibited and repressed by Revealed Religion are frequently those most essential to our survival. Hating an enemy drives us to act against that enemy and keep the enemy from further harming us. Praying to curtail our natural instincts and innate drives which enabled our ancestors to survive and produce us is a suicidal exercise.

Intelligent Morality replaces slavish prayer to nonexistent Gods with the goal of understanding and following the laws of Nature so that they assist us rather than oppose us. Our individual and collective organism is interconnected with the rest of Nature. Just as a bobcat sniffs the scent of its prey and follows its trail, our interconnection with environmental matter, energy and forces, and the past, present and future can guide us to success if we open our consciousness to it. This is a very esoteric and sophisticated subject that I will not further explain here. I only mean to reveal that there are superior methods to relate to and use the past, present and future than futile prayer.

Prayer can be useful for defining goals and achieving a direction in life for those who know no other alternative. Acting involves contemplation. One good idea can save years of work, prevent tragedy and change the course of a person's life for the better to an immeasurable degree. Sometimes waiting a week to learn more and come up with a good idea or find good advice can prevent decades or a lifetime of failure. Ignoring and avoiding bad advice can likewise prevent catastrophe.

A family, group or society dedicated to accumulating and sharing tested and proven useful knowledge, methods, skills, means, etc. will prevent countless tragedies and improve the quality of life of its members. Shakespeare's plays frequently portray the tragic consequences of deliberately bad or unintentionally misguided and bad advice and choices.

Chapter Six
Becoming Overly Risk Averse Is Itself Risky

Erring on the side of caution becomes Evil if it produces depression, neuroses, fear, anxiety, stagnation, crippling inaction, etc. Worrying about not making a mistake instead of acting to shape the future is highly destructive.

Intelligent Morality frees us from the anxiety that our actions will unintentionally produce bad results, because it acquires and accumulates the knowledge and data that greatly increase the probability of success. An Intelligently Moral society will elevate the level of goods and services so that its members will have far more confidence in the abilities of others and quality of goods and services. The streets will be far safer as will the hospitals and schools.

We should not fear risk, but instead minimize it when we can and accurately evaluate it when we cannot. Just as our actions can produce unintended bad consequences, they can also generate unexpectedly good results. Experimentation and risk taking are vital to success.

Chapter Seven
Are the Masses Ready for Intelligent Morality?

It is not necessary or moral to go down with a sinking ship. It is better to detach from people who are incapable of survival and unwilling or opposed to doing what is necessary to survive. Too much energy is today focused on educating and persuading others of the reality of our situation, rather than preparing for what the enemy has planned for us and finding ways to survive it. The enemy is very clever at using attempts to counteract it to its ultimate advantage. They have spent thousands of years developing strategies and methods to turn our weapons against us. We have to stop stepping into their mousetraps and reacting to what they have already accomplished and instead dedicate ourselves to building something new of our own and keeping them from ruining it.

I know their various plans. They have many alternative plans and there is no guarantee that they will pursue one or the other as events unfold, or that they will succeed. They will certainly always aim to exterminate us. It is their *raison d'être*. We should do what is in our own best interest regardless of what the actual outcome of the enemy's actions are. Even if the enemy totally fails, what we build will serve us well. If the enemy succeeds, we will, too, and the enemy's success will have unintended benefits for us, as well, that will enable us to eventually defeat the enemy and preserve our people despite their general failures. Unfortunately many of our own people serve the enemy even in the name of fighting it. We are not duty bound to destroy ourselves trying to save those who cannot be saved.

In a Good society, people are competent at their jobs be it work related, or being a parent, teacher, statesman, mate, etc. Incompetence regularly creates horrific and lasting Evil which is only resolved through death. We can start building a Good society immediately by modifying our own behavior and beliefs. Refrain from hurting or mistreating those you love. Search out demonstrably tested and proven methods and solutions before acting or making decisions. Act with care, patience and caution instead of impulsively or recklessly. Seek out knowledge and be skeptical and inquisitive instead of trusting or gullible. Pass along wisdom to your kids and grandchildren and treat them as the precious extension of your life that they are. Form networks and communities that are mutually supportive and provide job and school recommendations, career paths, introductions, etc. Keep track of who provides good advice, and who bad. Don't give advice which is not known to you to be proven to work without disclosing the fact.

Be careful which books, movies, songs, social media content, news, etc. which you allow to permeate your consciousness or reach your children and grandchildren. Media of all forms, as well as friendships and relationships, are highly influential both as bad influences or good influences most especially in the formative years of children.

We will save as many as we can and will encourage everyone to maintain banks of their seed and eggs. We will try to generally defeat the enemy in ways it has not anticipated and cannot counteract. But we will also build for ourselves and will not allow the failings of others to slow or drag us down. We will survive in spite of them if they continue to do exactly what the enemy wants them to do.

Chapter Eight
The Stealth War of Extermination

Our enemy employs ways of killing and sterilizing us which are essentially undetectable and against which there is no defense absent the knowledge of their existence, which they attempt to conceal. When this War of Extermination is exposed enormous efforts are made to render the subject taboo and damage the reputation of those exposing what is happening.

In order to defend ourselves against this existential attack upon us; which includes the poisoning of the food, soil, air and water with GMO's and toxins; as well as the promotion of usury, debts, miscegenation, open borders, invasion, unhealthy lifestyles and practices, derision and degradation, unnecessary and self-destructive perpetual wars and revolutions, corrupt government, destructive educational institutions, deadly and harmful medical practices, etc.; we must become aware of what is happening and learn how to stop it and cure ourselves. Good outcomes cannot be expected in a society under perpetual deadly stealth attack designed to inevitably eradicate its members.

Revealed Religion is one form of this stealth attack as in the case of Christianity and that of Islam. Replacing Revealed Religion, or at the very least supplementing Revealed Religion with Intelligent Morality, is an effective means of revealing what was hidden and developing methods to defend against the stealthy and deadly attack on our People.

Why hasn't Allah always protected Muslims from those who mass murder Muslims? Why hasn't Jesus Christ and the God of Israel always defended Christians from the Christian killers? The Gods of the Egyptians served them well until the Greeks stole them and gave the Egyptians Serapis. The Greek Gods made the Greeks rulers of the World until the Romans stole them. The Romans ruled until the Judeans captured their Gods and gave the Romans Jesus. There is something to this. Our ancestors' Gods have been stolen from us and in their place enemy Gods have taken over and are producing our demise by the enemy's deliberate design. The old national and tribal Gods were symbolic analogues for teaching our People how to survive and defeat our enemies, as well as uniting us. The enemy has stolen them and given us self-destructive Gods who instruct us to destroy ourselves and the world because we are supposedly conceived in Evil.

Political movements including Marxism, Secessionism, Revolutions, etc. are also stealth means to exterminate a people by pitting it against itself, gaining the reins of power and killing off the best and most productive members of society who sustain and improve the entire people. Intelligent Morality reveals that those beliefs which are deceptively claimed to be altruistic and philanthropic aspects of these Revealed Religions and Political Movements are instead demonstrably subversive and genocidal. Many historical examples provide the data which proves these facts. Once an Independent State is formed, the tables will turn. We, too, can be stealthy, undetectable and inevitably effective. The enemy set the precedent.

Chapter Nine
Safeguarding Your Immortal Soul

Every aspect of our being changes with each passing moment. If the Soul were truly immortal, it would be immutable, but it is not. In his autobiography, Geronimo wrote that he had watched many people die, some very closely by his own hand, and never once witnessed anything like what is described as the Soul or Spirit of the human being leaving the body upon death. Geronimo wrote,

> "IN our primitive worship only our relations to Usen and the members of our tribe were considered as appertaining to our religious responsibilities. As to the future state, the teachings of our tribe were not specific, that is, we had no definite idea of our relations and surroundings in after life. We believed that there is a life after this one, but no one ever told me as to what part of man lived after death. I have seen many men die; I have seen many human bodies decayed, but I have never seen that part which is called the spirit; I do not know what it is; nor have I yet been able to understand that part of the Christian religion."[1]

Our best assessment of our empirical observations to date indicates that DNA is the source of and model for our entire organism and existence. It passes to our children who are most likely to resemble us if we mate with someone with like DNA. The human brain produces our thoughts and sense of self. It is the product of our DNA. If our aim is to perpetuate that which Revealed Religion calls our "Soul",

---

[1] Geronimo, *Geronimo's Story of His Life*, Chapter XXII, "Religion", Duffield & Company, (1906), p. 207.

then Intelligent Morality demonstrates that it is imperative for us to safeguard, perpetuate and preserve our DNA by reproducing with those who resemble us and are a healthy and prime match, or find some technological means to replicate our DNA into new living organisms like us. It is also a primary concern to ensure that proper nutrition enables our DNA to form a healthy organism and to keep toxins, radiation and other harmful agents and elements out of our living environment and bodies.

These facts contradict the destructive mythologies of many Revealed Religions. For example, *Galatians* 3:26-29,

> "For ye are all the children of God by faith in Christ Jesus. For as many of you as have been baptized into Christ have put on Christ. There is neither Jew nor Greek, there is neither bond nor free, there is neither male nor female: for ye are all one in Christ Jesus. And if ye be Christ's, then are ye Abraham's seed, and heirs according to the promise."

The enemy and modern technologies employed for profit rather than long term survival have already modified our DNA with GMO's, radiation, vaccines, miscegenation, toxins, promiscuity, treating women as common property, dysgenic wars, open borders, etc. Inferior specimens are encouraged to breed with the best. There will be ways to reverse some of these effects and the graves of our ancestors must be safeguarded as a source of DNA for comparison, analysis and perhaps someday regeneration. Samples should be taken and carefully preserved.

Intelligent Morality will immediately enable many to safeguard their DNA from the short list of threats just named. There is much more to this that is better spoken of later in confidence.

Chapter Ten
The Impact of Technology on Human Evolution

Natural selection involves both the organism and its environment. Human beings have a tremendous capacity to alter the environment to facilitate or eliminate the potential for a specific type of, or generally, human life to continue. Your enemy may argue that if your race is dying out it is because your race is unfit to survive and Nature is running its course. This assertion is not necessarily or universally true.

It has been and is often the case that races are exterminated by environmental conditions which extinct races would otherwise have survived and prospered had not their environment been artificially or naturally altered in ways that produced their death, sometimes deliberately, as in the case of the destruction of American Bison to decimate the Plains Indians by removing their food source. They are attempting to take away cattle, poultry, eggs, milk and pork from European Peoples in the same way to exterminate us. Survival of the fittest includes the survival of organisms which alter their environment to make it fit for their survival, as well as those who change the environment of those they seek to exterminate to make their victims' environment unfit for their continued survival.

It is crucial to take into account that survival of the fittest involves the environment as well as the organism. A normal dolphin is fit to survive in the Pacific Ocean, but the Senora Desert is not a fit environment for a dolphin to survive. If left in the desert, the dolphin will soon perish. The destruction of European Peoples is due to their environment changing to become unfit for their survival, not an inability to survive in a fit environment.

This changed environment has occurred deliberately and includes the promotion of mass non-European immigration, European self-hatred, internal and external European wars, the acceptance and promotion of non-Heterosexual relationships, the promotion of childlessness and miscegenation, etc. A dolphin is not considered an unfit organism unworthy of survival simply because it cannot live in the desert. Europeans cannot be considered unfit to survive merely because they are being killed off by the deliberate destruction of their environment which includes the use of psychological warfare against them to make their mental environment and beliefs unfit for their survival.

Intelligent Morality compels us to study, acknowledge and condemn all of the Evil horrors that technology and those who employ it have wrought on the Earth and its creatures. Revealed Religions falsely teach humanity that we are children or creations of the Gods and have dominion over the Earth. This has fostered the reckless and inhumane use of technology in grossly immoral ways that have produced terribly Evil harm often in the name of doing Good and serving God.

On the other hand, primitive peoples and Luddites (those who shun technical advances and advantages) are at a tremendous disadvantage relative to a technically advanced society *that employs Intelligent Morality to ensure its survival, growth when necessary and self-interests.* But most if not all technically advanced societies are presently self-destructing as the Third World outbreeds and invades us. Under these conditions, technological superiority has again proven to be disadvantageous to the long term survival of our kind, but this is NOT a necessary result of technological advancement, but it is instead the product of greed, short term thought and deliberate subversion by the enemy.

The enemy has produced, proliferated and disseminated doctrines, laws and political ideologies which promote selfishness and the atomization of our peoples. In the fields of economics and business, the enemy has taught us that it is proper to exploit freedoms and loopholes in the Law to do deliberate harm as long as it is legal to do so, and to never be inhibited by moral, ethical or societal interests. They preach that it is the job of government to prohibit harmful conduct, and that if the government does not do so, private persons have no duty to safeguard society. This, of course, ignores the demonstrated fact that these same people corrupt the government to prevent it from barring their harmful conduct. They exploit the freedoms of our society to enslave us, because they view themselves as our enemy and are setting about to take from us everything of value and to exterminate us.

If this enemy force were purged or contained, and our society promoted the best interests of its members, we could enjoy our freedoms without becoming enslaved by those who deliberately use our freedoms to subvert us. The freedom to own firearms exists to protect us from those who seek to kill us, but is often exploited by those who wish to murder us. The enemy does the same with our Freedom of Speech. They use this freedom as an excuse to silence us, intimidate us, misinform and mislead us, defame us and corrupt society by privatizing and monopolizing the public square and demanding that the government recognize their Freedom of Speech so that they can take away our Freedom of Speech. Instead of banning Freedom of Speech, which cannot produce the desired end of freeing up speech for everyone as their fundamental right, it is instead necessary to penalize or remove the enemy so that we can enjoy our rights without their being employed as genocidal weapons against us. The enemy is to blame, not our rights which can be enjoyed in peace and harmony in a homogenous society that does not suffer from an internal existential enemy, Trojan Horse and fifth column subverting and destroying it.

It is not desirable to burn down the barn to get rid of the rats. Killing the patient does not cure them. Our ancestors always understood that an enemy should be treated as such and not tolerated or permitted the liberty to destroy them. Instead of banning liberty it is necessary to confront and defeat the enemy and separate from it.

The enemy created the technologically advanced thermonuclear weapons system of Mutually Assured Destruction between America and Russia and aimed it at all the traditionally European-based nations, so that we can all be exterminated at once by mutually killing each other off. The enemy instigated the technologically advanced wars which then enabled them to demand the production of these genocidal weapons which they designed, manufactured and tested in America. The enemy then betrayed America and gave the technology to our mortal enemies, their allies, in Soviet Russia.

The enemy has generated lower birth rates in developed countries by encouraging the destruction of the nuclear family, women in the workforce, homosexuality, birth control products, abortion, open borders increasing housing costs and lowering wages, high taxes, imports destructive of domestic industry, farming and labor, toxins, selfishness, greed, misguided individualism, etc. After creating the system of Mutually Assured Destruction of European Peoples, the enemy has created heavily hyped movies, books and other media to keep the masses in a constant state of fear and the European States at perpetual war and on the precipice of mutual annihilation.

Technology affords a tremendous competitive advantage as in the case of thermonuclear weapons versus spears, and airplanes versus horse drawn carts. As such, this technology is a double-edged sword. Those without nuclear weapons are at the mercy of those who possess them. Those who possess them are the likely first targets of others who possess them. And those who have both nuclear weapons and the means to prevent others from striking them with their delivery systems have the greatest edge afforded by advanced technology.

Many nations have taken steps to build nuclear shelters and to store food and other supplies, and some even keep a carefully guarded storehouse of seeds to replant after the anticipated global catastrophe. But none have taken any steps to create a bank of their citizens' male seed and female eggs to repopulate our kind in the event of a nuclear war, or in the event that the genetics of our race becomes so denigrated or miscegenated that it can no longer produce offspring that will survive, that resemble us, are procreative enough to maintain the population, or can no longer produce offspring at all. Why don't governments which send soldiers off to die in the prime of their breeding years first collect their male seed and female eggs so that their sacrifice does not result in the extinction of their line should they be killed? With all the talk of preserving diversity why aren't there banks of the eggs and seed of Whites given that studies show that the White populations are declining and their DNA is degenerating?

Intelligent Morality will lead us to not rely upon nonexistent Gods to repopulate our people in the event of catastrophe and to realize that it was not the Gods which created us in the first place. It is incumbent upon us to create banks of our human seed and eggs and to carefully safeguard them. If we are the only people to do this, then our artificially bred offspring after any form of calamity may be the only human beings to exist in the future after our current generations become unviable are destroyed and cease to exist. If it is necessary to preserve organic and non-genetically modified plant seeds as a means of restoring the plant kingdom following catastrophe, it is all the more important to preserve the best human DNA in the form of viable male seed and female eggs. This can be done eugenically, as well, to not only restore, but improve upon the races.

Instead of relying upon dissimilar immigrants to provide labor, professionals, soldiers, etc. and who threaten to become a hostile force which will outnumber and take us over, we can instead utilize Artificial Intelligence and robotics which can accumulate and assess data and surpass largely inept, overworked, arrogant and greedy professionals, and which can work continually and efficiently without any political power, corrupting cultural influence, self-interest, miscegenating genetics or contagious diseases. Robotics, Artificial Intelligence, domestic education and job training combined will solve the immigrant labor and services problem.

It is important to maintain genetic diversity, but self destructive to promote the reproduction of inferior stock and effective sterilization of the best. Eugenic selective breeding among humans will have the same beneficial outcomes it does among other animals. Artificial reproduction and cloning can quickly increase a waning and dying population in the event it becomes necessary. Technology has enabled the survival of very poor specimens. It also provides a means for cloning and artificially breeding superior specimens. Revealed Religion with its egalitarian mythologies of the Soul has discouraged Eugenics and encouraged the breeding of the worst genetic stock. Greed, selfishness and misplaced altruism have led to a drop in the birthrates of the best genetic stock.

Power, wealth and influence disparity bears an accompanying dysgenic incentive to lower the status, health, intelligence, well-being, financial security, education, etc. of the masses so as to increase the advantages, power and control that wealth and influence accrue for the wealthy and influential. This of necessity causes the leadership of society to think and act to the detriment of the majority of the members of the society, most especially in cases where the privileged are already foreign, hostile, psychopathic or otherwise mentally and morally ill. The greater the disparity in power, wealth and influence between the few and the many, the more dysgenic the institutions, laws, culture, religion, food supply, medical practices, marriages, mating practices, etc. are apt to become producing increasingly inferior offspring in every successive generation. In addition, the most successful are encouraged to become the most selfish and shun having children, which is also dysgenic. Dysgenic wars kill off the most courageous and aggressive prior to their passing along their genes to the next generation. Marxists deliberately murder the brightest and best to keep them from reproducing and leading and providing competition to the enemy.

Such societies often devolve into lower life forms. As the genius of the people diminishes it often imports foreign labor of low genetic quality that lacks the average high intelligence, morality and creativity of the ancestors of such societies. A point may eventually be reached where the once lower quality foreign immigrants are morally and intellectually superior to the degenerated natives and overtake the positions of authority, power, wealth and influence. The old race is then subjugated, assimilated and disappears. Such societies are inherently immoral because they are degenerative and extinctionist. Morality compels survival.

Technology has afforded the enemy the opportunity to lower our birthrates and alter our genetics in destructive and harmful ways. Technology also enables those with obvious genetic defects to survive, mate and pass along their genes.

An Intelligently Moral society will advance learning and make available tested knowledge and proven facts. Intelligent Morality recognizes the tested and proven fact that gross power, wealth and influence disparity is dysgenic, degenerative and ultimately destroys the people who tolerate it, including those who increase it in the name of fighting it, such as the Communists who always establish an absolute Plutocracy that rules over masses of absolute slaves.

Chapter Eleven
A New Society

Instead of falsely viewing the present situation as if hopeless and descending into defeatist self pity, we should realize and exploit the many opportunities it affords us. The general state of man is rapidly degenerating. Testosterone levels have dropped. Birth rates have fallen. People are becoming more easily manipulated and controlled. Societies are increasingly more authoritarian and employ ever more advanced and restrictive technologies to oppress and tyrannize the increasingly inferior masses. Careers and jobs are becoming obsolete. Food sources are being eradicated. Geoengineering and countless other factors are destroying the living environment of the Earth and human genetics. Etc. Etc. Etc.

That means that a select core of eugenically selected men, women and children that simply preserves their unique and superior DNA, qualities, attributes and numbers, even without doing anything else, could gain an ever greater and accelerating advantage over the masses of humanity who are being deliberately destroyed and diminished. If on top of that natural advantage we already enjoy, we employ methods of selectively mating and breeding and develop advanced technologies, an advanced culture, Intelligent Morality, robotics, Artificial Intelligence, Weapons of Total Destruction, superior and more nutritious foods, a healthier local environment, detachment from and alienation of the enemy and its weapons, etc.; then we can gain ever greater and more rapidly advancing advantages over our competitors and enemies. Intelligent Morality frees us from the religious burden to go down with the sinking ship of the gullible, stupid and subverted masses who try to cling to us and drag us down with them as they descend into oblivion by our enemy's design. Eugenics can select against the genetically defective, weak, stupid, disloyal, psychopathic, insane, treacherous, gullible, inept and corrupt.

Admission into the New Society will be highly selective and discriminatory most especially so after it is firmly established. At the same time, genetic diversity must be preserved and Nature has demonstrated the benefits of variety.

Robotics can provide the labor we will need. Artificial Intelligence can supplement the professions and assist in everyday life to help us to avoid bad decisions and inform us as to potential tested solutions to many problems.

It is not the purpose of this foundational book to reveal my plans in specific detail. To do so would be counterproductive and serve the enemy. Rather, I am pointing out that the situation is by no means hopeless and affords us the opportunity to advance humanity while surviving the enemy's exterminatory attack on us all.

Judaic, Christian, Islamic and Marxist mythology plan for a chosen elect to inherit a New Earth and New Heavens, which is called the "World to Come". The wicked will all perish leaving the World to Come exclusively the domain of the righteous. That's the common plan that is being carried out today and all these faiths have been deliberately engineered to produce the same ultimate outcome—our demise.

The enemy's actions and intentions afford us with the opportunity to surpass them and inherit the Earth they are tragically cleansing of the rest of humanity. They are inhibited by their plan, which I alone have fully deciphered and successfully used for 30 years to predict world events with 100% accuracy. My track record is public. I know precisely what they have planned and how to use that knowledge to survive and thrive. I am the only person who possesses this priceless treasure.

Chapter Twelve
Weapons of Total Destruction & Ultimate Deterrence

Thermonuclear weapons are not enough to deter the enemy. In fact, the enemy created nuclear bombs with the intent of using them to destroy humanity as they go underground to their hellish new Noah's Ark to survive the nuclear holocaust they have engineered for us. We need weapons which are capable of removing the entire Earth from existence, or to end *all* life upon it with absolute certainty, in order to effectively deter our genocidal enemy. We need Weapons of Total Destruction, not merely Mass Destruction. We also need defensive systems and shelters in which we can survive their intended Apocalypse should they ever succeed in inflicting it upon us.

During the Cold War, so-called "Doomsday Devices" were proposed which were land-based and stationary bombs. Such a device would not require a delivery system and would be virtually impossible to preemptively or preventatively destroy. A large enough thermonuclear bomb or set of bombs salted with sufficient quantities of Cobalt that would become Cobalt-60 upon detonation could theoretically effectively destroy most human life on the planet with sufficiently massive radioactive clouds raining radioactive particles over large enough portions of the Earth to ultimately produce the extinction of most of the human race.

Our enemies are quietly and secretly working on what I refer to as next generation "Weapons of Total Destruction" (as opposed to lesser Weapons of Mass Destruction). Particle physicists are attempting to detect theoretical subatomic particles and forces at supercollider particle accelerators. Their research could potentially be used to create what I term "Black Hole Bombs", "Subatomic Bombs", "Abyss Bombs" and "Implosion Masses". If this technology succeeds in creating microscopic Black Holes it will pave the way for one type of next generation Weapons of Total Destruction which are literally capable of eliminating the entire Earth and converting it into a Black Hole.

It is theoretically possible to condense Mass into such an intensely condensed form that it will produce something similar to the theoretical "Black Hole". This could create the next generation Weapon of Total Destruction. Nuclear bombs progressed from simple single stage fusion Atomic bombs which are generally in the 15 to 25 kiloton yield range capable of destroying dense cities with a population of one quarter million or less, to the far more destructive multi-stage fission-fusion thermonuclear weapons.

The Abyss Bomb will be an Implosion Mass and will have the exact opposite effect of a nuclear chain reaction one stage fission Atomic Bomb. Instead of exploding atoms, it will implode them into rapidly growing Black Holes which will be fed more Mass until they consume one another and the entire Earth. Instead of producing a fission or fusion reaction, the Implosion Mass will instead condense Mass and feed the growth of an intense local gravitational field with additional Masses such that the accretion of the microscopic Black Hole greatly exceeds its decay and evaporation. Upon activation, the Earth will consume itself into the nothingness of ultimately dense and immutable Mass.

The problem which once led many to conclude that Atomic Bombs were impossible was the need to accelerate radioactive decay to the point where the energy was released from the atom in a short enough span of time to produce a massive explosion. The problem was solved when Otto Hahn demonstrated a nuclear chain reaction. Abyss Bombs pose the opposite dilemma of the supply and continuous accretion of Mass at a far greater rate than the decay of the microscopic Black Holes and the production of stable particles which resemble theoretical microscopic Black Holes.

I do not adhere to current particle theories, relativity theory, string theory or quantum mechanics, but the language of these current models of theoretical physics suffices to convey the gist of the potential for such a Weapon of Total Destruction. I have developed a new Physics which appears to me to be logical, internally consistent, falsifiable by experiment and account for all known phenomena, as well as alternative models and plans for Abyss Bomb devices which may produce these potential effects without the use of super collider particle accelerators through the employment of what I poetically call stable "Devil Particles" and "Satan Forces".

A study of safety concerns at the Large Hadron Collider (LHC) concluded that there is NO potential risk from theoretical microscopic Black Holes forming during their particle collisions should they indeed be produced.[2] I will not disclose my insights and research for obvious reasons and it remains unreviewed and untested. My purpose in revealing the existence of this research is to sound the alarm of the danger this will pose to us should our enemies

---

[2] LHC Safety Assessment Group, *Review of the Safety of LHC Collisions*:

https://lsag.web.cern.ch/LSAG-Report.pdf

sufficiently develop such technologies before us. I am also exposing these secrets to demonstrate the potential for producing Weapons of Total Destruction which will serve us as the ultimate deterrent to the enemy's aggression against us as a means of defending our New Society from them and their inevitable genocidal attacks.

Research which is ostensibly conducted to redirect asteroids and comets so that they do not strike the Earth or to use their gravitational field to deliberately change Earth's orbit around the Sun to reduce surface temperatures, could as easily be used to aim them directly at the Earth so as to cause a catastrophic event like that which theoretically may have caused the extinction of the dinosaurs. A massive enough mass striking the Earth at such high velocity would certainly produce tremendous damage through a variety of effects. The enemy's expressed intent is to destroy the world. This is another possible means for them to do it with a Weapon of Total Destruction. Be very careful what research you sponsor or engage in even in the name of saving the planet. It may very well be used by the enemy to destroy it and us.

I also have plans for biological, chemical, environmental, atmospheric, radiological, energy and other forms of deterrent Weapons of Total Destruction, as well as delivery systems and plans to scuttle the enemy's development of these weapons. Like it or not, the race is on to be the first to produce such weapons and it is to our advantage to inhibit our enemies' work and advance our own research and self interests. Enough said—for now.